THE ART ROM

I ♥ DOGS & PUPPIES

Created by the Top That! team

Published by Tangerine Press,
an imprint of Scholastic Inc.
557 Broadway, New York, NY 10012.

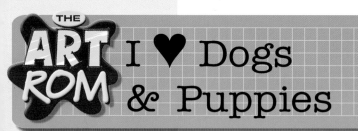

THE ART ROM
I ♥ Dogs & Puppies

If you adore dogs, then you'll love the fun-filled projects that come with this amazing book and CD-ROM. The CD-ROM is easy to use and the book explains exactly how to use it, in simple step-by-step instructions. Learn all about dogs and puppies and their behavior, how they communicate, where they live, and much more!

Themed Projects

There are 16 projects for you to make using the cool images from the CD-ROM. Once you have chosen your favorite image from over 500 pictures you can get started on these fantastic activities:

• Impress your pen pals with your very own customized stationery.

• Decorate your bedroom with a hanging picture mobile.

• Brighten up someone's day with grr-eat gift ideas and projects.

• Transform plain and boring household objects into works of art with découpage.

I ♥ Dogs & Puppies

Doggie Heaven

Print the images from the CD onto acetate and make a light catcher to brighten up your windows. Decorate a pencil box, "Do Not Disturb" sign and a letter rack and you'll be in doggie heaven!

Find Out More

As if that's not enough, there's also information about how you can find out more about dogs and puppies.

So what are you waiting for? Start making some projects!

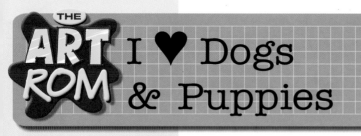

I ♥ Dogs & Puppies

Dogs and puppies are our best friends. They play an important part in ancient Persian and Chinese religion, folklore and mythology. Images of the dog appear in art forms all over the world. They are faithful, caring, understanding, playful, lively and interesting. Dogs are our favorite pets, making us feel happy, loved, important, as well as making us laugh. We like stroking them, grooming them, and playing with them. However, we shouldn't forget that dogs are animals and they have to be treated with respect, like humans.

I'M IN THE DOG HOUSE...

Happy Birthday

Pack Hunters

Dogs are carnivores and belong to the Canidae family. Closely related to wolves, dogs also used to be part of the bear family up until about 10–20 million years ago. Dogs are pack hunters, willing to work with humans and other dogs to capture prey. Dogs can hear sound four times farther away than humans can.

I ♥ Dogs & Puppies

THE ART ROM

Sense of Smell

Smell is a dog's most advanced sense. Touch is also a powerful sense, but their sight and taste senses are not as good as humans. They are perfectly coordinated and very active. Dogs use scent to mark their territory and attract a mate.

Different Breeds

Different breeds of dog are used for different things according to their characteristics. For example, greyhounds race, collies herd sheep, huskies pull sleds, and St. Bernards rescue people.

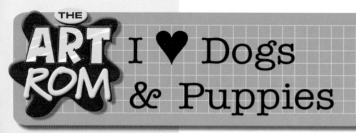

THE ART ROM

I ♥ Dogs & Puppies

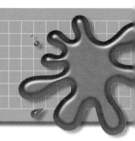

There are over 400 breeds of dog, from pure-bred to mongrels. Dogs are easiest to train when they are puppies. They are invaluable in performing all kinds of duties, such as leading the blind, sniffing out drugs, tracking scents, finding people after avalanches and earthquakes, finding injured soldiers on the battlefield, and detecting mines.

Famous Dogs

Some famous dogs include: Scooby Doo, Lassie, Beethoven, Mutley, Toto, Snowy, Clifford, Lady, Tramp, Gnasher, Timmy, Fang, Fred Bassett, Snoopy, and Hooch.

User Guide to CD-ROM

FOR PC USERS

The program should run automatically. If not, double click on the "my computer" icon on the desktop, and then on the "CD drive" icon. Then double click the title "art-pc.exe."

FOR MACINTOSH USERS

Double click on the "CD" icon on the desktop and then double click the title "art-mac."

MINIMUM SYSTEM REQUIREMENTS

Screen resolution 800 x 600
CD-ROM color depth 24 bit (true color).

- **PC USERS** – Intel Pentium® 166 processor running Windows™ 95/98 or NT version 4.0 or later, 32 MB of installed RAM, and a color monitor.

- **MACINTOSH USERS** – Power PC 120 Macintosh® running system 8.1 or later, 32 MB of installed RAM, and a color monitor.

NOTE: When you start up the CD, choose your preferred language to read it in by clicking on the flag.

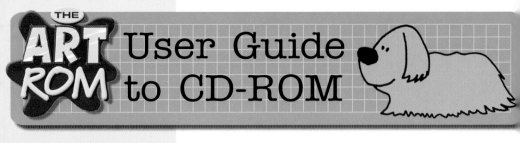

CD TIPS

To help you understand your CD-ROM, this handy user guide will take you through designing your own dog letterhead.

I Love **Dogs & Puppies**

Open File

Stationery

Picture Mobile

House & Home

Gift Ideas

Exit

1 First, choose the stationery section from the main menu.

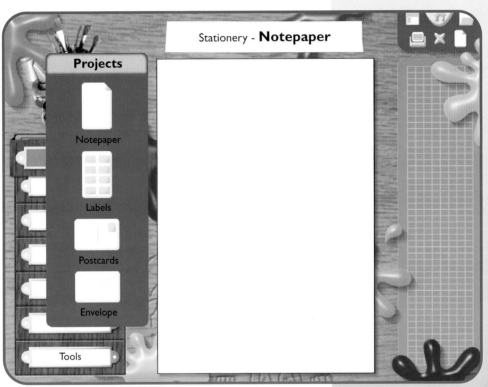

Stationery - **Notepaper**

Projects

Notepaper

Labels

Postcards

Envelope

Tools

2 You are going to design notepaper, so click on the "projects" drawer and choose "notepaper." You must close one drawer by clicking on it before you can open the next.

THE ART ROM
User Guide to CD-ROM

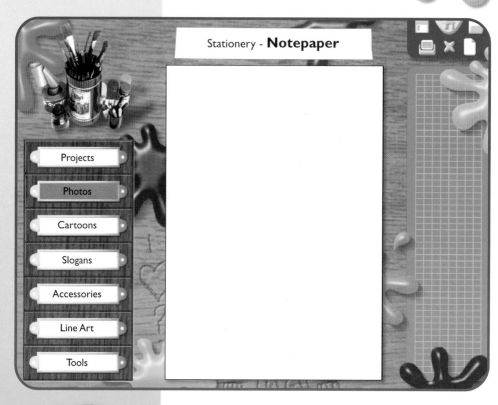

Stationery - **Notepaper**

Projects

Photos

Cartoons

Slogans

Accessories

Line Art

Tools

3 Next, add a picture. You can choose from photos, cartoons, or line art pictures. To choose a picture, simply click on either the "photos," "line art" or "cartoons" drawer. Don't forget to close a drawer when you've finished.

User Guide to CD-ROM

Projects

Photos

Cartoons

Slogans

Accessories

Line Art

Tools

4 You will notice that the pictures are in a grid, and at the top of the screen are left and right arrows and text, indicating how many pages of pictures there are and what page you are on. Use the arrows to move through the page of pictures until you find a picture you want to use.

ART ROM

User Guide to CD-ROM

Projects

Photos

Cartoons

Slogans

Accessories

Line Art

Tools

5 To make your choice, click on the picture and you'll notice that it appears on the green pasteboard to the right. You can have up to eight pictures at a time on the pasteboard. Remember to close the drawer when you have finished what you are doing.

User Guide to CD-ROM

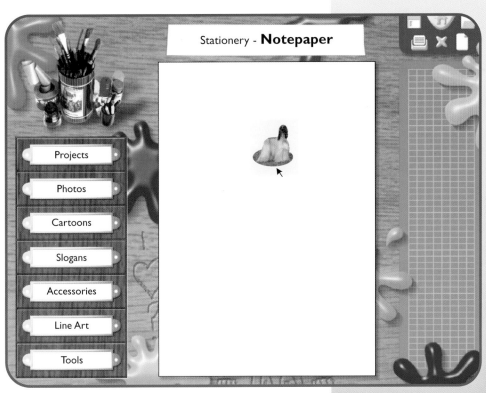

Stationery - **Notepaper**

Projects

Photos

Cartoons

Slogans

Accessories

Line Art

Tools

6 Drag the picture onto the page. Do this by clicking on an image that you want to select, which will turn yellow. This means the picture is still highlighted and can now be altered. Still holding the mouse button, move the image onto your chosen position on the page.

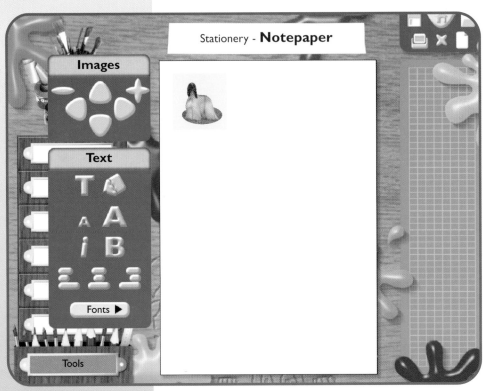

Stationery - **Notepaper**

Images

Text

T

A A

i B

Fonts ▶

Tools

7 To flip the picture, click on the "tools" drawer, then click on the left/right arrow to flip it left or right, or the up/down arrow to flip it upside down. You'll notice that there are "+" and "−" buttons, which you can use to make the picture larger or smaller.

User Guide to CD-ROM

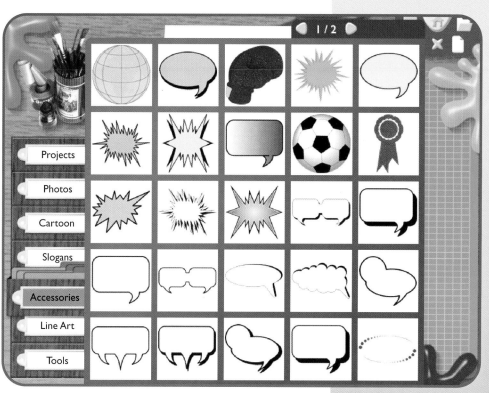

8 You may want to add accessories to the picture, using the "accessories" drawer. You can add items to the picture, such as a hat, cell phone, or a microphone. To add speech bubbles to the picture, click on the "accessories" drawer, then choose the image that you want and click on it. Move the image into position on the page.

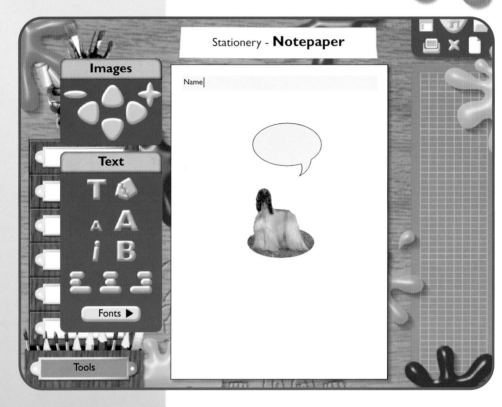

Stationery - **Notepaper**

Images

Text

Fonts ▶

Tools

Name|

9 Now you can add your name and address. Open the "tools" drawer, then click on the big "T" and you should notice a yellow bar appear on the page. This is where you do your typing. Type in your name and address, then click anywhere on the page to enter the text. To move the text around on the page, highlight it by clicking on it, then drag it to where you want it on the page. Any time you want to enter text or a picture, simply click somewhere elseon the page. The yellow will then disappear. You can have five text boxes at a time on a page. If you try to put more on, an alert box will appear.

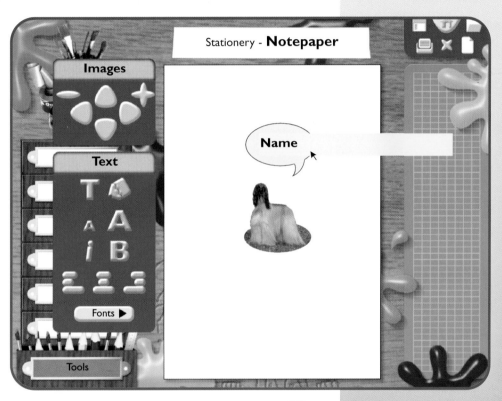

10 To alter the text, highlight the area of text you want to change by clicking on it. To make text larger, click on the big "A" button and to make it smaller, click on the small "A" button. To make the text bold, click on the big 'B' button, and to italicize the text, click on the "i" button. To align the text to either the left, right or center, click the align icons (see page 19).

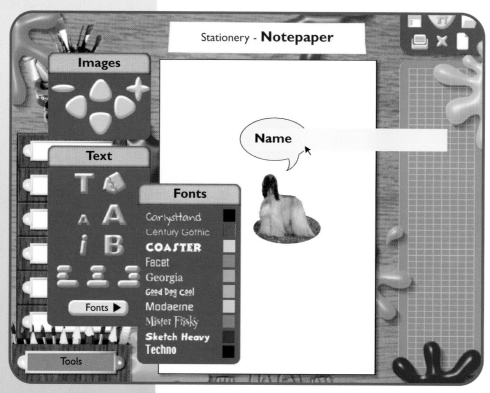

Stationery - **Notepaper**

Images

Text

Fonts

CarlysHand
Century Gothic
COASTER
Facet
Georgia
Good Dog Cool
Modaerne
Mister Frisky
Sketch Heavy
Techno

Fonts ▶

Tools

Name

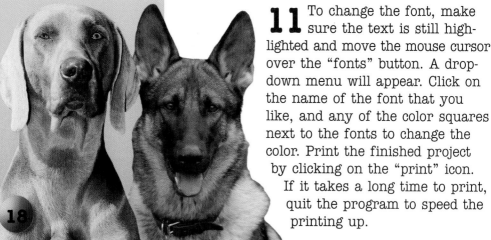

11 To change the font, make sure the text is still high-lighted and move the mouse cursor over the "fonts" button. A drop-down menu will appear. Click on the name of the font that you like, and any of the color squares next to the fonts to change the color. Print the finished project by clicking on the "print" icon.

If it takes a long time to print, quit the program to speed the printing up.

User Guide to CD-ROM

ICONS EXPLAINED

Click on the "home" icon to get back to the main menu.

Click on the "X" icon to delete a single picture. Just highlight a picture, then click on the X to delete it.

Click on the "page" icon to delete the whole page. When you start a different project after just finishing one, you have to delete the images from the pasteboard in order to start again.

Click on the "print" icon to print your work at any stage.

These icons are the "align" icons. This icon will align text to the left when you click on it.

This icon will align text in the center when you click on it.

This icon will align text to the right when you click on it.

Save your work at any time by clicking on the "save" icon in the top right-hand corner. Give your file a name when you save it and choose a place to save it, such as the desktop. To resave it, click on the "save" icon again. You will have to retype the file name in order to save it again. An alert box will pop up, asking you whether you want to replace the original or not. Click "yes" if you have a PC, and "replace" if you have a Mac.

Open a file by clicking on the "open" icon. Create a folder to save it in, and you can put as many documents in as you like.

19

PROJECT ONE
Notepaper

Decorate your letters with great growlers! Personalize your letterheads, envelopes, labels, notes and thank-you letters with your favorite dog images.

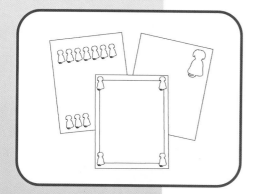

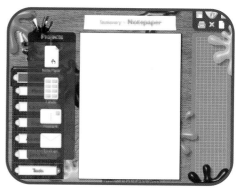

1 First, decide how you want your designs to look. You could use a border across the top and bottom of the paper, a border around the whole page or a simple letterhead design.

2 Go into the "stationery" section, then click on the "projects" drawer and choose "notepaper." Follow the User Guide at the beginning of the book to help you design your notepaper correctly.

3 When you are happy with the designs, print them out to see what they look like. If you like what you have created, print out several copies of each design. Your notepaper is now ready to use.

You will need:
- scissors
- glue

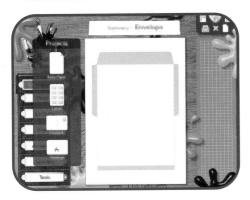

1 In the "stationery" section, click on the "projects" drawer and choose "envelopes." An envelope template will appear.

2 Choose your images and position them on the top half of the template. You can move the images around until you find the best position.

3 Print out the envelope template and carefully cut it out. Glue the gray parts together to make the envelope. Your envelope is now ready, so get writing to all your friends!

You will need:
- a sheet of eight white sticky labels

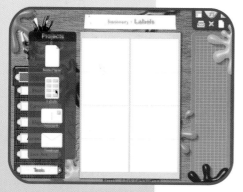

1 In the "stationery" section, click on the "projects" drawer and choose "labels." A template with eight labels will appear.

2 Choose an image and drag it into place on the template. You can add text if you want to, such as "To" and "From."

3 Print onto the sheet of labels. You can buy these from any computer or stationery shop. Attach to a gift or package, and neatly write who it is for, and from, on the label.

Postcards

You will need:
- thin cardstock
- scissors

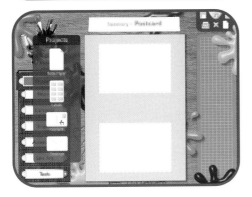

1 In the "stationery" section, click on the 'projects' drawer and choose "postcards." Two postcard templates will appear.

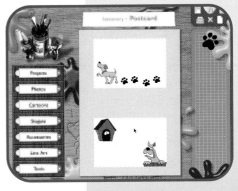

2 Click on a selected one or two images, and drag them into position on both the templates.

3 Print the postcards onto thin cardstock, cut them out and send to all your friends!

This great mobile is easy to make and looks fantastic wherever you hang it!

You will need:
- a pencil
- a paper plate
- thin colored card
- scissors & sequins
- a needle
- colored pens
- a marker
- a spool of thread

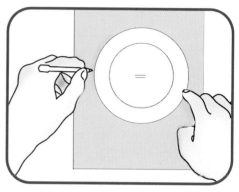

1 Draw around a paper plate onto a sheet of colored card — the diameter should be approximately 8 in. (20 cm). Ask an adult to carefully cut it out.

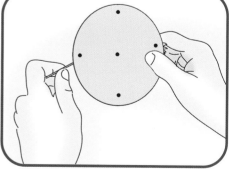

2 Make five marks on one side of the circle, as shown. Ask an adult to pierce each of these points using a needle.

24

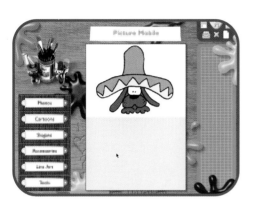

3 Go into the mobile section from the main menu. A blank page will appear, with a gray section on the bottom half. Choose some images and drag them onto the page. You can have up to four at a time, but one large one at a time might be best. Place them anywhere on the top half of the page.

4 You can also change the size. For example, you might find you want to make them quite large. Use the "+" and "−" buttons to increase and decrease the size. Click on the "print" icon and the image will automatically invert. This page will be the preview. If you are not happy with the image, click on the "back" button, change the image, and click "print" again to view the page.

25

PROJECT FIVE
Dog & Puppy Mobile

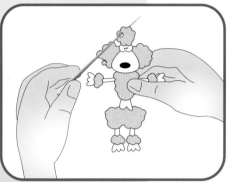

5 When you're happy, print the page and fold it in half. Cut the image out and align the pieces together, printed side out. Ask an adult to pierce holes in the images.

6 Use a piece of thread to measure the circumference of the circle. You will need to cut out a piece of card slightly longer than this length to go around the circle. You can make the depth as shallow or deep as you like, but remember to add an extra half inch along one edge for the tabs to attach it to the circle. You can decorate each mobile holder differently — use your imagination.

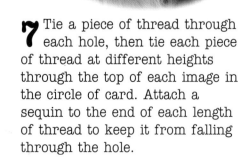

7 Tie a piece of thread through each hole, then tie each piece of thread at different heights through the top of each image in the circle of card. Attach a sequin to the end of each length of thread to keep it from falling through the hole.

8 To hang the mobile up, ask an adult to make three, evenly-spaced holes around the edge of the cardboard band with a needle. Thread three even lengths of thread through these holes, securing on the inside with a sequin. Then tie the threads together, from the outside, in the middle, and hang the mobile up. This is easier than tying them from the inside, because the mobile would tilt and not hang well.

Gift Box

Design your own gift box, wrapping paper, cards and tags for special occasions.

You will need:
- scissors
- a gift box
- glue
- a paintbrush
- paint

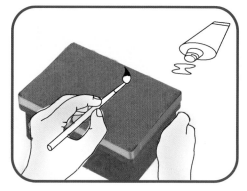

1 Go into the "gift ideas" section from the main menu. Click on the "projects" drawer and select "gift box." Select one or two images from the CD and print them out. Carefully cut them out.

2 If you want to change the color of your gift box, carefully paint it and let it dry. You can also cover it with wrapping paper instead of painting it.

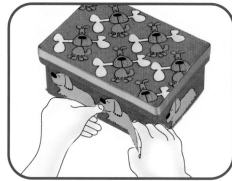

3 Glue the images onto the box and, when the glue is dry, put the present inside. Tie it up with some ribbon, or add a glittery bow.

PROJECT SEVEN
Gift Wrap

You will need:
- colored paper

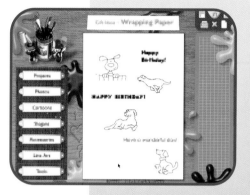

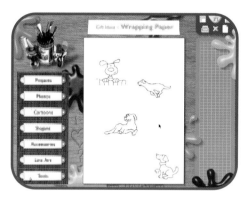

1 Select "wrapping paper" from the "projects" drawer in the "gift ideas" section in the main menu. Choose some images and position them onto the page. You might decide to have one image repeated, or several images.

2 Add text if you want, such as "Happy Birthday" or "Have a Great Day!" Why not try repeating the name of the person you are giving it to, in different fonts and sizes?

3 Print as many sheets as you need to wrap your presents.

THE ART ROM

PROJECT EIGHT
Gift Tag

1 Select "gift tag" from the 'projects' drawer in the "gift ideas" section in the main menu. Drag one or two images onto the gift tag template. You may have to make them pretty small to fit.

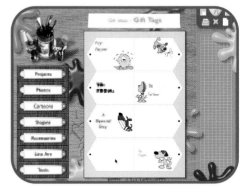

2 Add text, saying "To" and "From."

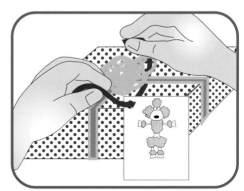

3 Print the tag onto the cardstock, cut it out and attach it to the present that is wrapped in the matching gift wrap or matching gift box.

PROJECT NINE
Greetings Card

You will need:
- colored cardstock
- colored or plain paper

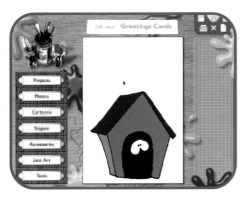

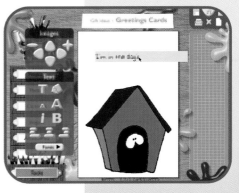

1 Select "greeting card" from the 'projects' drawer in the "gift ideas" section from the main menu. Choose some images and position them on the greeting card template.

2 Add text using the "tools" button. You could make it a themed card, or it could just be to say hello to a special friend! Print out onto thin cardstock or paper, and it's ready to write in.

Happy Birthday

I'M IN THE DOG HOUSE...

PROJECT TEN
Money Holder

Découpage (which means "cutting out") can transform all of your old things into delightful doggie or puppy objects! When you glue, paint or varnish, always make sure you do it in a well-ventilated area. Wear old clothes and put lots of newspaper down first. You may need an adult's help.

You will need:
- a plastic dish
- scissors
- sticky putty
- glue

1 Go into the "house and home" section from the main menu. Click on the "projects" drawer and select "découpage." Select several images and drag them onto the page. Print them and cut them all out. Stick the pictures randomly onto the money holder or box with sticky putty.

2 When you're satisfied with the overall look of the money holder, glue the pictures on. Keep your trinkets or old coins in it. You'll have saved up enough for a rainy day in no time at all!

Decorated Box

You will need:
- a clean box
- scissors
- glue
- a brush

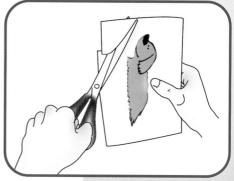

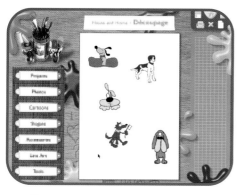

1 Go into the "house and home" section from the main menu. Click on the "projects" drawer and select "découpage." Select several images and drag them onto the page.

2 Print the images and carefully cut them out. Position them on the surfaces of the box in various designs until you're happy with the effect. Stick the pictures on with glue, making sure to smooth all the edges down. Let it dry.

3 Dilute some glue with water, and then varnish the box completely. You may need to get an adult to help you with this. Let it dry, then recoat at least two more times. This will give it a waterproof, shiny effect.

PROJECT TWELVE
Bookmark

You will need:

- scissors
- colored cardstock
- glue
- sticky-back clear plastic film/book covering

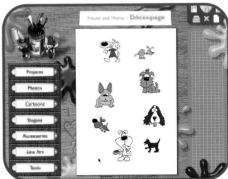

1 Select "découpage" from the "projects" drawer in the 'house and home' section. Print an assortment of about eight different images from the CD. Cut out a piece of card, about 8 in. x 3 in. (20 cm x 7 cm). Cut each picture out and arrange them on the card.

Bookmark

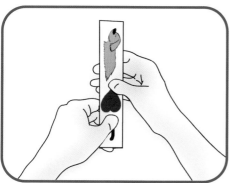

2 Stick half of them onto one side of the card. Let it dry and then stick the rest on the other side. When the other side is dry, cover both sides of the bookmark with clear sticky film.

3 Cut off any excess film, and get rid of any air bubbles by smoothing the film down to finish your bookmark. What a perfect gift for your friends!

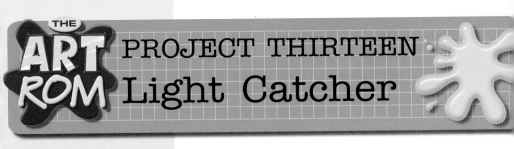

THE ART ROM

PROJECT THIRTEEN
Light Catcher

Use acetate paper to make a doggie or puppy light catcher and to decorate bottles and jars.

You will need:
- acetate sheet
- scissors
- a needle
- ribbon

1 Go into the "house and home" section from the main menu. Click on the "projects" drawer and select "light catcher". Choose an image and drag it onto the page.

2 Make it big, using the "tools" button. Print it onto a sheet of acetate and cut it out, leaving a 1-in. (2.5-cm) border around the edge.

Light Catcher

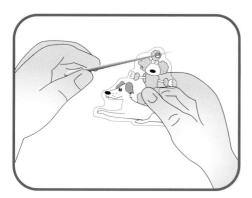

3 Ask an adult to pierce a hole in the top of the cut out with a needle, then cut a length of ribbon and tie it into a bow. Stitch it to hold it together. Cut another length of ribbon, tie in a loop and stitch to the bow. Thread the ribbon through the hole. Hang the light catcher up near a window, for a brilliant effect.

4 Or you could print out an image onto acetate and make it really big. Cut it out and stick it to your window so that the light streams through. You could make a cardboard frame for it as well, perhaps in the shape of a dog or puppy.

PROJECT FOURTEEN
Pencil Box

Decorate your room using techniques from the other projects. From a "Do Not Disturb" sign to a garbage can. Turn your room into a giant dog or puppy wonderland!

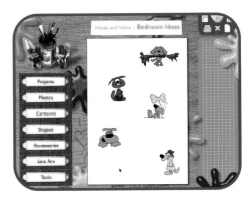

You will need: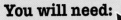
- scissors
- a box
- sticky putty
- glue
- a brush

1 Select "bedroom ideas" from the "projects" drawer in the "house and home" section. Select a few images and drag them anywhere on the page.

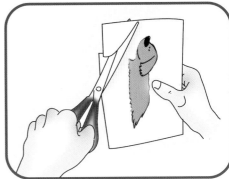

2 Print them at the size you require. Now carefully cut them out.

PROJECT FOURTEEN
Pencil Box

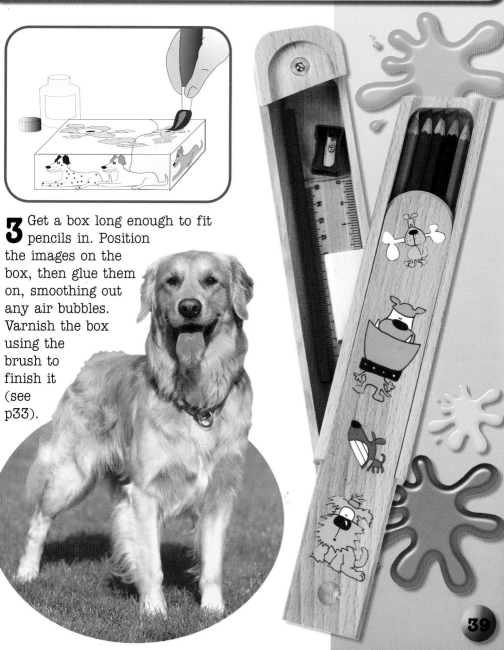

3 Get a box long enough to fit pencils in. Position the images on the box, then glue them on, smoothing out any air bubbles. Varnish the box using the brush to finish it (see p33).

PROJECT FIFTEEN
'Do Not Disturb' Sign

You will need:
- thick cardboard/ colored cardstock
- scissors
- a paintbrush
- paint
- glue
- a marker/colored pens

1 You can either use cardboard and paint it, or colored card. Cut out a shape of a sign. It can be in the shape of a dog, or just a square, but it must have a hook so that you can hang it over your door handle.

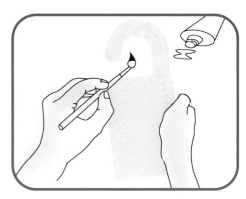

2 Now paint both sides of the sign if you are using cardboard, maybe using different colors for each. Allow both sides to dry completely.

40

3 Print a few images from the CD, then cut them out. Glue them to the sign, making sure to leave space in the middle. With a marker or pen, write on one side "Go away," "Out," "Sleeping" or any other phrase you like.

4 On the other side, write "Come in," "Awake" or another phrase. Hang the sign on your door. You could also make one as a door nameplate.

You will need:
- a letter rack
- scissors
- sticky putty
- glue
- a brush

1 Select "bedroom ideas" from the "projects" drawer in the "house and home" section from the main menu. Select a few images and drag them onto the screen.

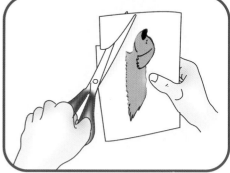

2 Print them out at the size you want. Carefully cut them out.

PROJECT SIXTEEN
Letter Rack

3 Position the images on the rack with sticky putty until you're happy with your designs. Glue the images onto the letter rack. Varnish them with diluted glue.

43

There are many ways in which you can find out about dogs and puppies. There are lots and lots of books and journals that you can find in any library and bookshop.

You could ask an adult to help you search for dog websites on the internet.

If you are lucky enough to have a dog or a puppy, make sure you look after it well and give it lots of exercise. If your dog is misbehaving, try taking it to a dog-training class.

If you don't have a dog, perhaps you could offer to help walk your friend's or neighbor's dog. Sometimes elderly people need someone to give them a hand walking a dog, and sometimes people will hire youngsters to walk their dog if they're ill or going on vacation.

If you want to work with dogs and other animals, visit a kennel one Saturday afternoon and offer to help look after dogs by washing, feeding, or grooming them.

Pictorial Index

This pictorial index contains all the images on the CD. You can use it to quickly find which picture you're looking for without having to go through the CD.

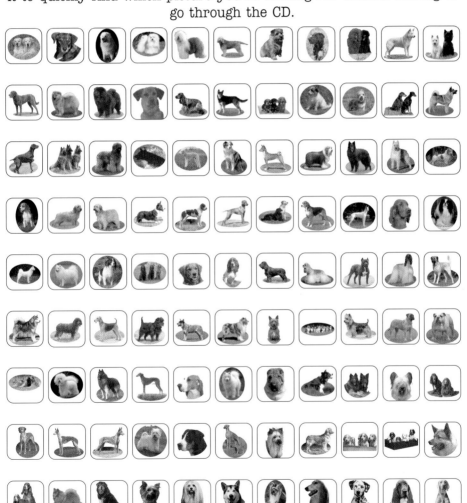

 # Pictorial Index

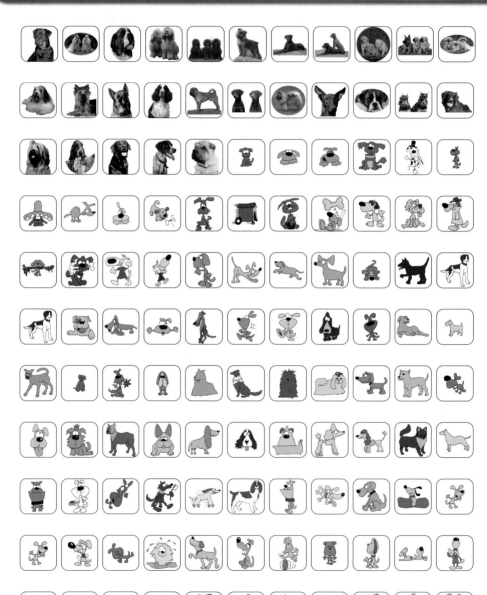

Pictorial Index

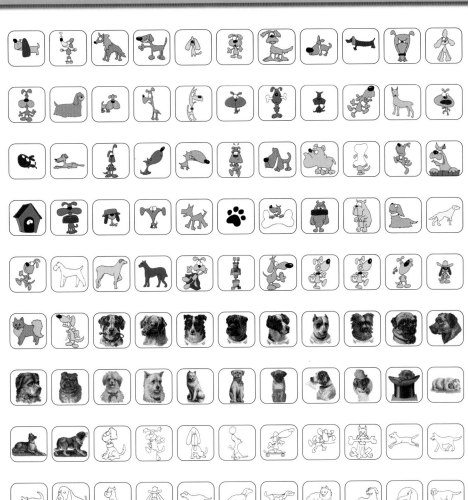

Pictorial Index

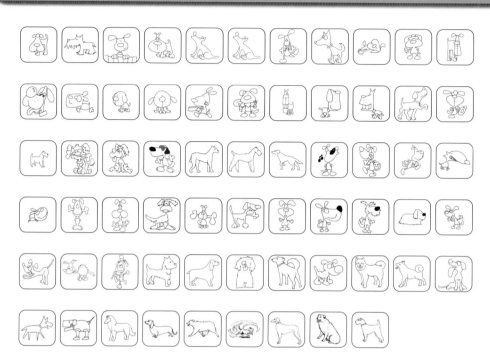

You can choose from these images,
as well as other accessories and slogans.